The Secrets to Your Business' Success

The Guide on How to Double Your Money

By: Ronan Knightly

9781635010329

PUBLISHERS NOTES

Disclaimer – Speedy Publishing LLC

This book was originally printed before 2014. This is an adapted reprint by Speedy Publishing LLC with newly updated content designed to help readers with much more accurate and timely information and data.

Speedy Publishing LLC

40 E Main Street, Newark, Delaware, 19711

Contact Us: 1-888-248-4521

Website: http://www.speedypublishing.co

REPRINTED Paperback Edition: ISBN: 9781635010329

Manufactured in the United States of America

DEDICATION

I dedicate this book to everyone who has the guts to take the challenge and make a legacy in any business field.

TABLE OF CONTENTS

Publishers Notes.. 2

Dedication 3

Chapter 1- Business Planning: Research and Feasibility Study... 5

Chapter 2- Business Planning: Collating Pertinent Information . 9

Chapter 3- A Compressive Tip on Starting Your Business Right
....12

Chapter 4- Keep The Positive Aura Flowing 20

Chapter 5- Apply the Check and Balance Principle.........27

Chapter 6- Be Committed and Stay on Track....................34

Chapter 7- Be A Great Leader and Attain Business Success........39

About The Author..49

Chapter 1- Business Planning: Research and Feasibility Study

You've probably heard the old cliché: "He, who fails to plan, plans to fail". There's a great deal of truth to this slogan. Those who are successful in business don't shy away from creating strong business plans.

But there are also times you don't have a choice, whether or not you feel comfortable about it: You have to create a business plan. For example, you're applying to join a government program and submitting a business plan is one of the requirements... or you want to expand your business, but you need a bank loan. In the latter case, submitting a detailed business plan is paramount.

Business plans come in all shapes and sizes... from ones scribbled on napkins to ones that look like dry, thirty-page legal documents.

Which type of business plan is right for you and your business today?

The Secrets to Your Business' Success
Step 1. Determine What Type of Plan You Need

Your goal in creating a plan in conjunction with where your business is "at" right now will dictate what type of finished product you end up with. Before you can determine this, however, familiarize yourself with the more common types of business plans...

1. Start-up Plan – This type of plan outlines the new operation, introducing the company as an entity. It typically covers and introduces areas such as:

• The industry or niche the business serves

• The product(s) being produced

•A mission statement

•An executive summary

•The market and its demographic data

•Method of operation

•Forecasts for future growth

•Projected sales and profits

•Financial data such as cash flow sheets and balance sheets

•Start-up costs and projected operational costs

•Milestones already achieved

•Team members – both management and workforce

• Appendices

This list may seem daunting if you're new to business plan creation, but remember that several of these sections can easily consist of a short paragraph each.

Creating a start-up plan provides a solid, well-defined structure for your business, even if you are the only person who is ever going to see it. It will give you a realistic overview of your business and make it much easier for you to plan and move towards your goal.

2. Feasibility Study – This type of business plan is almost always required if you are seeking government, bank or business-organization-funded start-up grants or loans.

It includes many or all of the elements in a start-up plan, but market analysis should play a major role, as well as projected costs and expenses.

Its purpose lies in determining whether or not the proposed business is going to be viable. The question it should answer is: "Does this candidate know what she is talking about?"

3. Strategic Plan – A strictly internal plan, this one is all about prioritizing and goal-setting. It might be included in a company manual or distributed to management. It normally cuts out window-dressing such as mission statements and financial data, focusing instead on actions that need to be taken, in order to get the company from A to Z.

4. Operations Plan – This is the type of plan you would create annually. It is used as a road map, and normally includes data such as steps to be taken over the year, projected implementation

dates, deadlines, and data such as which department, team and supervisor is responsible for each step.

5. Internal Plan – This type gives more of an overview. It can be very down-and-dirty, if it is meant to serve a specific stage of growth or step in the company's planning… or it can be a "snapshot", meant for the company manual.

6. Expansion Plan – This type of plan can be internal or written for potential investors. It needs to be as specific and thorough as possible if used for the latter purposes, including data such as:

•Mission Statement

•Executive Summary

•Organizational structure

•Sales

•Profits and losses

•Projected growth

•Projected expenses

A business plan is not a set-and-forget document that sits forever unchanged, cast in stone. It is a business aid you can revisit and revise. Business plans are a necessary part of your strategies.

Over the lifetime of your business, you may create many different types and versions of your company business plan. Learning how to create one quickly and effectively – ones that include only data relevant to that plan's particular purpose – will serve you well.

CHAPTER 2- BUSINESS PLANNING: COLLATING PERTINENT INFORMATION

Where do you find the data you need... particularly information that hasn't even been created yet? And how do you decide:

• Which information you can leave out

• Which information you absolutely must include

The latter is easy: Suit the sections you include to that particular business plan's purpose.

As for the former – finding the data you need – there are many easy ways to do this; both online and off.

1. Create Surveys – Online and offline surveys provide a wonderful starting point for finding out what your target audience wants, what they're willing to pay, what their problems are, what they want most urgently; what's not being provided.

Offline surveys could be as simple as getting permission from your local mall's management and accosting people with a clipboard; asking customers who visit your physical store to fill out a short survey; including a short written survey on a stamped postcard with a regular physical mailing or simply asking people at business functions, club meetings or at industry fairs or events. This type of firsthand research is called "primary research".

Online surveys are easily created with apps and online software, often provided for free. Try SurveyMonkey, which provides possibly the easiest way in the world to create your own highly-effective, online custom survey.

All you may ever need is their basic free plan – especially if you just want to provide impressive-looking data for start-up business plans. And don't be intimidated if you glean only a handful of responses. As long as the respondents accurately represent your target market and you are up-front and truthful about your numbers, you can impress potential investors with even small surveys.

What surveys say to backers is that you actually took the time to poll your target market and glean real-time data and feedback.

2. Visit Online Statistics Sites – You can also collect impressive and accurate statistics for your business plan by visiting statistics sites such as Alexa – When this powerful stat site's home page opens up, simply type the keyword or name of a specific online company you would like data for in the Search box.

If you are presenting data to a nuts-and-bolts investor such as a bank manager or government agency case manager, you can often impress the heck out of them with detailed data from stats sites such as Alexa. Believe it or not, many of these investors don't know how to easily glean industry data, and automatically assume you spent days collecting and assembling such data – when all it took was a couple of clicks!

But the bottom line is that your data will be truthful and accurate.

Study Your Competitors

There are other ways besides stats sites to study your competitors.

Visit your local Chapters store or supermarket and head for the magazine section. Find the sub-section that specifically covers your niche. Take note of:

• How many magazines for your niche

• Top headlines (these are your hot topics)

• Industry experts and celebrities

• The advertisements for products (particularly noting prices)

Once you have a thorough understanding of your industry's facts and figures, you'll be in a strong position to add it to personal information you already know (such as where your business is going to be located; what type of products it will sell, et cetera) to start creating your powerful, targeted, unique business plan.

CHAPTER 3- A COMPRESSIVE TIP ON STARTING YOUR BUSINESS RIGHT

Business Plan - Step-by-step Instructions for Creating

You're ready to create your business plan... or are you? Here are the basics you need to have in place.

Step 1. Define Your Business

You have a good idea of what you want your business to do. You've done preliminary research and identified your target market. You know what type of business model you want; whether it's retail or trade, service-based or product based. So how would you explain your business, if asked to do so?

Many people find themselves hemming and hawing at this point. You know what it's all about, but it's a little hard to sum up.

If this sounds like you, you're not ready to sit down and put your plan together. You need to define your business model the way a diamond cutter perfects a diamond.

Ask yourself the following questions:

• What does my business do?

• How does it do it?

• Who does it serve?

• What "gap" does it fill?

• What is unique and special about my business?

• What is my business' strongest advantage for its clients or customers?

It may be a trifle outmoded, but after you've done this, think "elevator speech". Imagine stepping into an elevator and bumping into someone who asks you what your business is all about.

What would you answer, in three lines or less? How would you strip away all irrelevant detail?

How would you summarize your business?

Step 2. Write your Mission Statement

One of the best ways to create your elevator speech lies in writing out a mission statement for your business.

This doesn't just explain what it sells or what it does: It encapsulates your company's core values, beliefs, ethics, goals and purpose.

The best way start writing: Look at examples of other company mission statements.

These can be as short as a simple sentence, tag line or slogan... or comprise more than one paragraph: However, mission statements should try to get to the heart of your business as clearly and directly as possible.

Let's take a quick look at a sampling of effective Fortune 500 company mission statements:

• "To make the world's information universally accessible and useful" – Google

• "To be America's best run, most profitable automotive retailer" – AutoNation, Fort Lauderdale, FLA

• "To discover, develop and deliver innovative medicines that help patients prevail over serious diseases" – Bristol-Myers Squibb Company, New York, NY

• "Create value for shareholders through the energy business" – Kerr-McGee Corporation, Oklahoma City, OK

• "Mattel makes a difference in the global community by effectively serving children in need. Partnering with charitable organizations dedicated to directly serving children, Mattel creates joy through the Mattel Children's Foundation, product donations, grant making and the work of employee volunteers. We also enrich the lives of Mattel employees by identifying diverse volunteer opportunities and supporting their personal contributions through the matching gifts program."

• "To bring inspiration and innovation to every athlete in the world" – Nike Inc., Beaverton, OR

• "Our business is pharmaceutical care. Our mission is positive outcomes" – Omnicare, Covington, KY

• "We fear change." – Wayne Campbell, Wayne's World, movie; 1992

When writing your company mission statement, follow these tips:

1. Be as clear and direct as possible

2. Avoid clichés and overused phrases like "culture of diversity" or "with particular emphasis on"

3. Cut out adjectives and adverbs, which weaken your prose. If a sentence doesn't work without adjectives and adverbs, split it into shorter sentences and rewrite completely

4. Cut out unnecessary words. This includes filler phrases such as "Be that as it may" and "unlikely though it may be".

5. Show how your company benefits the community, shareholders and/or the world

Step 3. Decide Which Type of Plan You Need

Who is it for? What effect does it have to have on them? Do you need to provide projections for a Feasibility study? Are you attempting to show how financing would bring a successful return to a bank or investor?

Decide which of the following plan types will best serve your purpose at this time...

• Start-up Plan – For your own clarification; or for presenting to potential investors or backers

• Feasibility Study – As above; plus more in-depth market analysis and projected costs and expenses

• Strategic Plan – Strictly internal; all about actions that need to be taken. May be included in a company manual

• Operations Plan – Annual road map containing implementation dates, deadlines and responsibility allocation

• Internal Plan – Overview or snapshot, to be included in the company manual

• Expansion Plan – Similar to a Feasibility Study. Detailed report aimed at investors, banks and backers. Includes profits and losses, projected growth and expenses, opportunities and steps for expansion

Step 4. Assembling Your Data

Make sure you have all the data and research you need completed and at hand. This can include:

• Survey results, scans and screenshots

• Industry statistics

• Statistics from any split-testing you may have done

• Market research results

• Sales figures

• A balance sheet

• Other financial data

• Your mission statement, slogan and/or tagline

• Graphic files containing your company logo, in .JPG or .PNG format

• Headshot .JPG or .PNG

• Any other relevant photographs in .JPG or .PNG file, including a snapshot of your premises; headshots for any key personnel or staff members

Step 5. Use a Template

If you've never created a Business Plan before, your best bet is to use a template. You can either obtain a sample of an existing plan (online or from your bookkeeper or a friend with a successful business) or model your own on that one or you can download an actual blank 5emplate (recommended).

Step 6. Start Writing!

Once you've assembled your data, create an outline before you ever enter a word of body text. This will help you create a well-balanced plan that is neither missing any sections nor focusing too much on one particular section.

If you are using a Template that already provides you with a structured table of contents and outline, you can simply start filling in your body data straight away.

Ditto, if you are using an online wizard.

If you are writing from scratch, however, it is vital to create your outline first. In any type of business plan, your headings should include:

• A cover page, with your logo and who the Plan is for

• A Table of Contents (TOC)

• A Mission Statement

• Executive Summary (if applicable)

After that, add or include sections as needed, depending on the type of plan you intend to create.

Step 7. Proof Your Plan

When you have finished your business plan, run a spell checker on it. Go through the results carefully and make any corrections. Then save your plan, and put it away for at least a day.

Next morning, read through it. Correct any errors and highlight klutzy sentences you want to rework.

Congratulations – you have now completed your first business plan. Just remember that business flans are never static: They are living, breathing roadmaps for your growing – and successful – business.

Chapter 4- Keep The Positive Aura Flowing

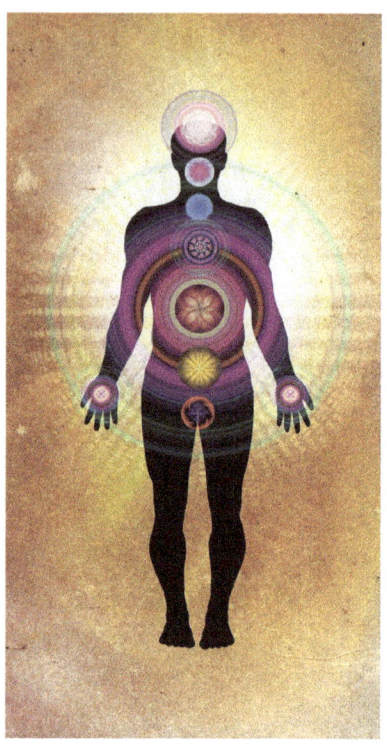

Whether you are new to business or not, you shouldn't underestimate the term "organized". Being organized is a foundation of being productive.

When you say organized, it doesn't mean that you have to clean your office or other essential things. Being organized has a broad and extensive scope. The real organization is a mental state and describes on how you think.

If you want to be organized, you need to spend enough time dealing with your stuff and learn how you can approach your work more effectively. To know more about the mentality of being organized, you can read the following paragraphs.

Top 5 Tips on How to Be Organized

To become organized, you don't need to follow any complicated task. Instead of worrying on how to do this, here are the top things you need to do:

1. Understand that being organized is not just about trying to get more items sort out. It also doesn't mean that you can't tactically buy some stuff that will help you become more organized. To become organized, you need to start in improving your state of mind.

2. To become organized, you have to consider stuff according to its purpose. It means that you don't need to keep things that are useless. You also need to ensure that your stuff has its own value. Say for instance, you don't need to keep your tables around your office if you are not using it.

3. Another best way to become organized is to know your priorities. If not, you will never know what you really want. It is also impossible for you to reach your specific goals, both personal and business concerns.

4. To become organized, you have to figure out the real you. Most business owners don't know how to define themselves. Some of them are also afraid to admit who they really are. But, if you are willing to accept the real you, you can easily know what you need to do and what you really want to achieve.

5. To get organized, you need to get all the things that are valuable to you. So, make sure that you get rid of the things that are not important to you. Then, start organizing the valuable things that you have.

The Secrets to Your Business' Success

Sorting out your business stuff is easy to do. Once you became an organized person, you are doing what you really love and your actions reflect to your personality. So, if you don't want some distractions, it is best to get rid of unwanted stuff. You also need to separate your identity from the items that you own.

If you don't know where to start from, you can start making your resolution. Just make sure that you will follow your resolutions whatever it takes.

Methods on How to Keep Up with Training

Creating a business resolution is quite fast and easy. The main tricky is its actual implementation. If you want to maintain your business resolution, regular practice is advised. However, how can you do the training if you are quite busy?

Though you are too busy, you can still change for the better. You can achieve your goals through showing that you are eager to reach it. With regular practice of your business resolution, you will soon realize that you are doing it naturally.

However, not all businessmen understand the significance of training. Some of them decide to skip their training, especially when they have an urgent meeting or event. Whether you have lots of things to do, you can still practice your business resolution. You just need to adjust your schedule and know your priorities.

To maintain your business resolution, you need to practice it every day. For your guide, here are some methods you can do to ensure that you are doing the right and effective way:

• Make Your Own Schedule – Once you already knew what you really want to do, you have to create an effective and attainable schedule. Simply jot down what you need to do every day and make sure that you follow it accurately.

• Don't Make Excuses – To become a successful business owner, you have to focus on your goal. If you already made your own resolution, you have no choice but to follow it. Though you are busy with your work or family life, you have to set things right. You have to guarantee that you will practice your resolution no matter what it takes.

• Don't Make Shortcuts – Businesspeople make resolutions to improve their daily operations. They are also doing this to ensure that their business is getting better compared to the previous years. If you want to become a successful businessman, don't forget that there is no shortcut way of success. Therefore, you have to start at the bottom up to the peak of your success.

Training plays a vital role to reach your desired goals. At first, you may say that you will do the training because you are following your resolutions.

But, as time passes by, you will do the training like an ordinary activity.

So, instead of worrying about your business, start making a resolution and follow it accurately. Then, expect that you will get the fruitful result of your hard work.

Yes You Can

To overcome the different challenges of your life, you have to think positively. Instead of worrying about your flaws and insecurities, you need to face them. You have to keep on practicing the "I Can Do It" mentality.

The "I Can Do It" mentality plays vital role in your life. Whether you are facing simple or complicated challenges, you are certain that you can overcome it. You just need to believe in yourself that you can do it.

This "I Can Do It" mentality means that you have to eliminate all your negative thoughts. Though some people keep on saying that you can't do it, use it as a challenge. Never underestimate yourself because everyone has the power to reach an ultimate success.

If you are practicing this kind of mentality, it means that you need to eliminate excuses. So, don't let excuses get in the way of your goals. You have to focus on your dreams and achieve them through your positive thinking.

However, some people claimed that it is impossible for them to achieve success. Even if you commit mistakes and failed several times, it doesn't mean that you will never be successful. Don't look at a failure at something negative. These flaws and failures can be used as your strength and way to do things better. Just don't let failure hold you back.

How Achieve "I Can Do It" Mentality?

Most people claimed this common phrase – "It is easier said than done". This statement is extremely true. Even if you want to think positively, there is always a time that you will think negative thoughts. The main question is how can you avoid negative thoughts and start practicing the "I Can Do It" mentality?

There is no complicated step in achieving the right mentality. At first, you need to focus on long-term goals. You also need to remind yourself of your blessings and strengths. As advised, don't allow yourself to get into a spiral of negative thinking. When your negative thoughts arise, make destructions and start thinking with positive ones.

In addition, you also need to maintain a good relationship with others who have a positive mentality. This allows you to become more optimistic. You can also write down evidence of opportunities and positive activities every day. You can do this through making a journal.

Stay on Course

Positive affirmations are often used to impress the subconscious with a thought that can motivate and remind you about your talents. It also provides the confidence you need to reach your goals, business resolutions and other missions.

With regular use of positive affirmation, you can easily change your attitude, habits and behaviors. You can also use it to heal and find prosperity and romance.

Negative thoughts can be altered by using positive affirmations. If you don't know how to do it, you can use the following guides:

1. Decide What You Really Want - You just need to think about your life and the things that you want to have. Say for instance, if you want more money, use this as affirmation. Just be clear about your goal and do everything to achieve it.

2. Use the Present Tense when Making Affirmations – Most people make affirmations like "I will be a successful business". This statement claims that you will soon to be a successful businessman. To encourage you in reaching your goals, you have to say that "I am a successful businessman".

3. Always Be in Positive Mode – Whether you are speaking or writing your affirmations, don't forget to use positive phrases. Say for instance, if you want to get a high monthly sale, you need to say that "I Can Do It".

4. Always Remember Your Affirmations – To get what you really want, you have to repeat your affirmations several times. You also need to believe in yourself that you can easily do it. Then, you will realize that you are one step closer to your goal.

5. Be Persistent – Affirmations only work if you used them regularly. The more frequently you repeat your affirmations, the longer you say them. As a result, the quicker you will achieve your ultimate goal.

To make your affirmations stronger, you need to make them bold, clear and positive. When you start doubting your affirmations, don't forget to realize that your non-conscious brain is transmitting you a signal based on your conditioning. Above all, you have to keep recommitting to the process to get a successful result.

Take note that affirmations take some time. However, once you start its actual process, you will be surprised with its quick results. At first, you will feel like you are spending too much time and effort.

But, as time passes by, you will realize that the process begins to take over. So, all you need is to understand how to use your conscious faculties to strike into the phenomenal power of your non-conscious brains.

CHAPTER 5- APPLY THE CHECK AND BALANCE PRINCIPLE

Balancing work and family life is a challenging task. However, achieving its stability encourages the improvement of valuable skills. If you know how to balance work and family life, you can easily enhance stronger family relationship while improving your business operations.

To balance your work and family defines that you have to give an equal attention to both areas. Creating this balance does not often come naturally and it requires discipline and organization. When it comes to work and family concerns, not all business owners don't know how to balance them. In fact, some of them sacrifice family events to attend business meetings.

Steps-by-Steps on How to Balance Work and Family Life

Balancing work and family life promotes mental and physical health. It also enhances your ability to be organized. To give you some hints, here are the different steps on how to balance your work and family life:

Step 1: Make a Realistic Expectation – The most essential ways to balance your work and family life is to realize that you are just a human being. It means that you don't have the ability to do everything all at once. As advised, you have to prevent setting unrealistic expectation. If not, it will end up to disappointment. Say for instance, if you may not be able to attend the school activity of your daughter, you don't have to feel guilty.

Instead, make a realistic goal by adjusting your schedule.

Step 2: Make an Ideal Schedule – The easiest way to track your work and family activity is to make your own schedule. Therefore, you have to write down all the things that you need to do. You also need to pick a huge calendar or poster board to track your commitments and special events.

Step 3: Prioritize Your Family – Whether you are too busy or not, you have to prioritize your family. However, it doesn't mean that you will spend most of your time with them. Depending on your choice, you can set a schedule when to hang out with them without sacrificing your business commitments. As advised, you can watch a movie together or play an outdoor game during your free time.

Step 4: Learn When to Say "No" – If you have a busy schedule, you should not allow other people to distract you. You have to follow your schedule. You also need to say no to go to work events if it means giving up too much time away from your beloved family.

Step 5: Leave Your Work at the Office and Focus on Your Family While at Home – As much as possible; don't bring your work at home. If you did, you will never spend a quality time with your family.

Instead of worrying at home, take time to bring the whole family to mall or other entertaining centers. You can also make creative ways for your children.

By following these multiple steps, you are confident that you can easily balance your work and family life. Therefore, you will never sacrifice anything to have a perfect and wonderful life. Just make sure that you know your priorities in life.

Importance of Rewarding Yourself for Reaching Goals

Achieving goals takes time and effort. Whether you have a short or long- term goal, you have to ensure that you are doing the best move to reach it. Once you achieved your goals, it is best to reward yourself.

Rewarding yourself is a cool and easy way to keep you motivated. These rewards are something meaningful to you. They should be something you are willing to work for.

The reward system can be done in various ways. Like others, you have to pick a reward you desire after reaching your goal. Then, once you reached your goal, you need to reward yourself as soon as possible. Rewards come in various types. Depending on your choice, it can be a simple or elegant reward.

The Secrets to Your Business' Success

Why most people reward themselves for achieving their goals? If you don't know the reasons why, here they are:

• Rewards contour Your Behavior – Using rewards will turn your goals into habits. These rewards are also effective in maintaining a positive attitude. Rewards also make your daily transition into a healthy lifestyle. Therefore, rewards can help in developing your behavior and mental abilities.

• Great Tool for Motivation – Rewards allow you to stay on track. Whether you reward yourself a simple or grand stuff, it can help in encouraging you to continue succeeding. These rewards also give you something to work for. Then, once you achieved your goals, you will feel more contented and accomplished.

• Promotes Self-Confidence – Some people may underestimate your skills and potentials. If you continue to strive and achieve your goals, it can help in building your confidence. You can proudly say that you finally reach your goals. With rewards, you will feel good and allows you to celebrate your own success.

Rewards are something meaningful to you. They should be something you are willing to work for. To reach your goal, you should not use a reward that goes against what you are trying to accomplish.

Say for instance, if your goal is to improve your productivity, never reward yourself with something that would interfere with your daily routine.

The best rewards should reflect the importance and size of your goal. Then, you also need to use rewards if they mean something you personally. Say for instance, if you are not a big fan of English novel, never purchase a book as a reward. In addition, you should refrain from giving too much reward.

If you did, you will never focus on your goals, but to the reward itself.

As you can see, achieving any goal gives you a great and satisfactory feeling. Therefore, you should be excited about each milestone you reach. In some cases, the next step towards your goal seems even more challenging. But, when you think about the reward and longing to have it, this will motivate you to make a right move. So, start practicing the reward system and expect that you will get your ultimate goals in life.

Time to Enjoy You

Even if you are too busy with your work and family life, you have to take time for yourself. If not, you will be burned out. Too much work is not advised. That's the reason why you have to divide your time for work, family and for yourself.

For most business owners, they don't need to focus on themselves. Instead, they prefer to make miracles on how to reach their goals in life. Now, you can also do the same thing without pressuring yourself. If you keep on working and neglect to prioritize yourself, you will feel weak.

Giving yourself a time plays a vital role for your success. Some people enjoy a cool bath while others prefer to take a walk in a park. Whatever activity you want to do, you have to do it right away. Just make sure that you have to make plans.

To take time for yourself, you don't need to follow any complicated step. At first, you need to look at your calendar. Then, determine the best time for yourself. Before deciding, make sure that you finished your commitments to both work and family members.

After knowing your schedule, you have to save that day. It means that you need to block out a time where you can fit in a little rest and relaxation.

Then, you have to know what you want to do. Depending on your choice, you can join an exercise class or any activity. You can also watch some events in your local area.

To relieve your stress at work, you have to nourish your mind and soul. You can do this through meditation, listening to relaxing or slow music, and filing your minds with visions of youth. You can also breathe the fresh air, enjoy the sunshine or walk quietly in the woods. Though it is hard to do, you need to leave your problems behind for a little while.

Since you are taking time for yourself, it is best to be more relaxed while doing your preferred activity. In addition, you also need to nurture your body. To do this, you can get a massage to renew and rejuvenate body.

Depending on your choice, you can also make a healthy meal or take a relaxing bath.

Why do you need to take time for yourself? Taking time for yourself provides multiple benefits and here they are:

• Self-Reflection - This can help in developing your personal growth. This allows you to become aware of your experiences. If you reflect upon your life, you are also getting the wisdom to move forward. With self-reflection, you can decide what you want to do and what you don't want.

• Unplug from Society - Each day, people are surrounded by media. Some use social networking sites and televisions to get information. Through taking time to yourself, you will never attach to these different forms of media. It means that you will plug into your own thoughts, feelings and emotions.

• Self Influence – This is essential in your personal growth and development. Unlike others, you don't have to live your life influenced by the media. If you have time for yourself, you will know what you really want without considering the different desires of other people.

With great benefits of taking time for yourself, you have to make the right move. Start adjusting your schedule and witness how it changes your life.

CHAPTER 6- BE COMMITTED AND STAY ON TRACK

Business networking is an effective method for finding new customers and forging new business relationships. Contacts with different groups or clusters would help you in getting greener opportunities.

For most businessmen, the more diverse their network is, the better it would be. Once you attend group meetings, you have the chance to get the business cards of other business tycoons. As a result, that would bring a great business development.

Benefits of Networking in Business – What Are They?

Networking provides multiple benefits to business. This can help in expanding your contact list and improving your sales base. It can also bring you in touch with various requirements to diversify your company.

Unlike other business owners, you should always network. It is essential to make a lasting first impression on various people that you will meet. This impression you created will bring the better and wider business opportunities.

Just make sure that you always keep in touch with the contacts you have gathered. In addition, you also need to help people in your network. With this, you can easily bring not just goodwill but business improvement as well.

In networking your business, you should also consider on how to improve it. You need some insights about networking and relationship to guarantee business success. Networking helps the growth of your company. It is also effective in creating new products and expanding your ideas about the field.

Aside from the above mentioned, networking also helps in increasing your profits to a considerable degree. It also gives you the scope to get referrals and helps you to attain your targets in a fast and easy way. Networking also provides a healthy relationship and a mutually beneficial rapport with your competitors, compatriots, clients and suppliers.

If you want a successful business, you have to do the networking strategy. Through this, you will enjoy a steady rise in your balance.

If you are trying to excel professionally, you shouldn't miss to make a business resolution. Just make sure that you know what you really want and the exact things that you need to do to achieve it. With a successful business resolution, you can change your life in an instant. What are the benefits of making a business resolution?

The Secrets to Your Business' Success

The following will give you enough hints about the different benefits of business resolution:

Motivation

Making a business resolution is an effective way of boosting your level of motivation. This provides a sense of urgency to the work that needs to be accomplished. With this, you will be tempted to work in a fast and effective way. You will also not distracted with flaws and other related changes while reaching your goals.

Providing a Direction

Most people often find themselves wanting to change something in their lives. However, most of them don't know how to achieve it. With business resolution, they have a guide on how to do it. They just need to indicate what they want to achieve. They also need to know the different things they need to do to reach their goals.

Increased Success Rate

With accurate business resolution, you have a chance to improve your daily operation. As a result, you can easily know what are the things you need to do and the things that you need to avoid. Your resolution can be used as a tool to remind you that you can reach your goals. You just need to spend enough time and effort. Then, you will soon witness the prolific result of your hard slog.

Enhances Your Attitude

If you have a business resolution, you can easily control yourself. You will know your priorities and know how to handle your situation. Say for instance, if you keep on practicing your resolutions, you will soon realize that your daily routine is not the usual one. If you are not productive before, this resolution is an excellent guide to improve your work.

Get Organized

With the use of your business resolution, you will get organized. It means that you can manage your stuff and handles everything you need to do. You will also know how to balance your work and family life. If you are organized, chances to achieve your goals are extremely possible.

Limiting Stress

Your business resolution helps you in reducing stress. Without this guide, you may develop a tendency to jump from one project to another. Then, you may realize that your overall production is a mess. So, instead of worrying about your hectic schedule and tons of unfinished projects, try to make a business resolution and follow it professionally.

Stay on Track

Your business resolution is a roadmap to help you get where you are going. You just need to play out a plan to keep you headed in the right direction. To do this, you need to lists the steps you need to take and you will get what you really want.

Increased Self-Confidence

With your business resolution, you will do the right and best way to achieve your goals. Once you achieve it, more and more people will continue to praise you. You will also feel a great satisfaction and fulfillment due to your hard work.

The Secrets to Your Business' Success

With various benefits of creating a business resolution, most businessmen desire to have one. If you are one of them, you should make sure that you are following your resolution. If not, you will never get its full benefits.

Maintaining your business resolutions is not as easy as you think. But, if you know what you need to do and eager to reach your goals, everything will turn out great.

The success of your business resolutions relies on your hands. So, whether you have a simple or complicated resolution, don't worry about it. Try to focus on your goals. You also need to be ready and face the challenges while on process of achieving your goals.

Though it is hard to achieve, you need to focus on your goals. The main reason why you are making a business resolution is that you want to be better. To be better, you need to exert enough time and effort. Your success can never be achieved within a single wink of an eye. You have to earn it.

So, make a right move and see how your business resolution works!

Chapter 7- Be A Great Leader and Attain Business Success

Leading people has nothing to do with managing them. Too many managers are trying to micro-manage their staff, all the while forgetting to lead them effectively.

If you want to become a strong leader you need to lead by example. This means you have to show your team that you are perfectly capable to set examples.

By doing so you will earn their respect and create lifelong devotees who would move mountains to please you. Conversely, a manager who hides behind his office door while commanding staff isn't going to gain much respect in the work place.

Ultimately the success of any business venture lies in the hands of its employees and NOT the managers. A manager's responsibility is to organize and manage business systems, systems that will see to the successful finalization of projects.

If your staff is unhappy it will soon show in their lack of productivity. This will influence your bottom line. Chances are customer complaints will start to amass and office gossip will run hot. This is counterproductive to running a well oiled machine – your business.

No organization can function for very long without the co-operation of its employees. Unfortunately, the necessity in any organization is that there are various levels of status within the team, and this can lead to conflicts if not managed properly.

The effective leader has to realize that the team under them is there because they have to be. Most employees work to earn money, not because they enjoy the daily grind of a nine-to-five.

For this reason, there must be an effort to build healthy relationships, or life in the workplace can become untenable for everyone, and productivity will decline.

Leaders need to make their workplace society function positively, with co-operation and respect. In this way everyone is working for the common good and towards a common purpose.

This demands that effective relationships are built upon an understanding of each other's needs. It is no different to how things should be in the home; no personal relationship will last very long if there is a sense that one or both parties are being selfish.

The most effective way to understand how other people are feeling is to listen to what they have to say. This must be done without judging, and not as though you are being forced to do so by some higher authority.

Very often, teams will have the same goals as their leaders, but may just want to know that they are not seen as automatons that have no creative input.

Quality workplace relationships make people feel happy. One of the major reasons why employees move on from a company is because of relationship clashes with leaders or other colleagues.

Leaders should also make sure that they create the circumstances for understanding within their team, and this means asking questions. Assuming that your team will simply pipe up and express their feelings is not enough; many people will not feel it is their place to speak up unless they are specifically asked to do so.

Listening should be done attentively, not glancing at your watch every couple of minutes or trying not to look bored. This means you listen without interrupting or fidgeting, and with the correct expression. Your expression, by the way, should be genuine or you will be found out very quickly and the situation will become worse than had you not asked in the first place.

A great way to foster healthy relationships with your team is by meeting them in a more social environment on regular occasions. Some companies choose to send their staff to regular golfing outings while others prefer to host a monthly BBQ or weekend trips.

Regardless what you end up choosing, the key lies in giving your team a chance to connect away from the daily grind.

Building effective relationships means that neither party must make any assumptions. As a leader, you cannot expect people to understand exactly what we want and why you want it. Sometimes it is this lack of comprehension that causes problems.

As much as you must trust your team members to have intelligence, if they are not party to the goals you are working towards they can become resistant. As far as possible, your team should be conversant with your goals and how their actions are contributing to their successful outcome. Humans are inquisitive and function better when not kept in the dark.

Respect is the key ingredient of any good relationship, and this means respect for yourself as well as others. Genuinely listening and understanding are the ways in which you show that you respect the person you are talking to.

Quickly judging based on preconceived ideas or prejudice is the opposite of having respect. Bear in mind that not everyone will respond in 100% perfect fashion to all that occurs in the workplace.

Although it is not the leader's job to be a permanent shoulder to cry on, it is important to accept that your team is made up of individuals whose lives may not be as perfect as their coffee-break banter might lead you to believe.

Whilst creating a healthy working relationship is a crucial goal, the smart leader will always bear in mind that conflict is inevitable and must be managed, rather than ignored for the sake of apparent peace.

Relationships can never improve unless problems are identified and confronted. Differences between people are inevitable, and hearing them aired can lead to some very useful resolutions that produce ideas beyond the expected. The alternative is highly detrimental: to let problems fester and build, and ruin the atmosphere in a workplace, if not productivity levels.

Keys for success in working relationships:

1. One party at least should value the relationship – This may start off as a one-way street, but this can lead to a meeting of minds later on.

2. Listen effectively, without judging – Listening in this way will promote mutual understanding and mutual respect.

3. Have informal chats – Chatting over a coffee can encourage a more frank exchange of views than meeting officially with a desk between you.

4. Create an open culture – Your team should know they can speak freely, no matter if that is to express happiness, joy, contentment, anger, irritation, sadness or fear. Negative feelings that are hoarded cause significant problems.

Leaders must take responsibility for their team's performance, which means leaders must be happy that the direction of their team is one which the leader thinks is best.

Although it is useful to have creative sessions with team members to bat around a few ideas, the overarching goals that the team must fulfill are most often set by the leader, or some authority above the leader.

The challenge is therefore to get the team "onside" with the given aims, even when some team members may wholeheartedly disagree with them, or baulk at the idea that these have been imposed on them from above.

Despite the accepted hierarchy of any workplace, for a team to work most efficiently, its members – especially higher level ones – may want to feel they are contributing more than the spade work;

they may like to feel that they have chosen where some of the plots should be dug.

This presents a challenge for the leader who cannot just let his or her subordinates have free play. The team must be made to feel involved and motivated. Or perhaps the situation is worse, and your team is beginning to show a little disobedience. How then to provoke a positive response in them?

The answer is by empowering your team, as far as possible. Short of handing over the reins and heading off home, the motivational leader must be able to create a sense that their team is actively involved in the process and contributing in a real sense to the overall outcome of the project.

This can involve learning how to make your suggestions appeal to them. This may mean you solicit their opinions and take the best ideas on board. Or you may have to convince them that your goals are shared and that their futures are tied to your overall success. It may be a simple matter of making an employee understand that their job will be safer if they perform well; reminding them that they are working for themselves and their family, and not just for a company.

However, empowering others does not just mean employing tactics that persuade other people to your own opinion or goals. It can also mean demonstrating leadership qualities that inspire others to act at their very best, no matter what is asked of them. Such leadership qualities would be most in evidence in the armed services, where the end result of potentially being killed is rarely going to elicit a whoop and a cheer. Soldiers are empowered to greatness by the examples set by their commanding officers.

Sometimes, it is just a matter of being an admirable and inspirational human being. Of course, some are born with more of these qualities than others, but we can all strive to lead by example, so that others will feel empowered to make great things happen.

Getting the Most from Your Team Start right

When a staff member joins your team, give them time to become fully acclimatized to your company. The sooner they settle, the sooner you can start to reap rewards. It will help if you complete an induction and a detailed contract of employment, which outlines what you expect from them.

Create expectations

Strange as it may sound, some employees do not have a clear sense of their role. Such confusion can cause arguments, or even duplication or omission of tasks. This is clearly bad for productivity. Your team needs to know their job and responsibilities; a job description will help.

Stand back

Part of empowering your team is to trust that they can get on with the job without you peering over their shoulder every fifteen minutes. If you want staff members to flourish, they should be allowed to get on with their job. Of course you need to keep a watchful eye, but there is a happy medium where they know you trust them. Your team is more likely to over-perform if they feel good about what they are doing. Motivated staff works harder.

Money is often not the prime motivator. They want to know what is expected of them, and then they want to be allowed to get on with it. This is far easier if the right people are employed in the first place.

Communication

Effective communication is the lifeblood of any organization, regardless of its size. That may mean face-to-face talks or pinning notes on a board.

Provided your team knows what's going on, you are being an effective leader. Try asking your team how they prefer communication to happen. This helps to empower them.

Keep communicating

It can happen that there is a sincere intention to improve communication, and it all starts off positively: team briefs, newsletters; intranets, etc. Then things start to slow down. As a leader you should not let this happen. It may mean important information is not imparted, or you are viewed as not bothered how the team is getting on.

Be honest

Communication is not much use if your team believes it is not getting the whole picture. Bad news is still news, and you must trust that your people are mature enough to handle it, or you may find they are insulted and no longer believe what you tell them. This does not mean shouting every piece of office gossip from the rooftop, but it does mean keeping your team abreast of all that is pertinent to them.

Consultation

Effective consultation is a vital tool to improving performance. Your team members have specific roles. Your collective overview may be more knowledgeable, but there may be team members whose specific knowledge is greater than yours. Asking for their opinion is not weak; it is sensible, and it serves to empower that team member.

The more facts you have the easier and more effective your decision-making will be. Getting the most out of your team is greatly aided by effective consultation and it demonstrates respect from you to them.

Training

Training is a boon if it is relevant to the team members receiving it. You are guaranteed to alienate staff by sending them on courses that bear no relevance to their role.

Training for the sake of training is counter-productive. You need to ask: Will the training help the business? Is it geared to the priorities of the business? Are the right individuals and teams within your organization receiving the training? How can I quantify any improvement?

Training must be organized and delivered effectively or you should not commit to it in the first place. Ensure that the agreed priorities are met. Once this happens, think how you can help individual team members in their personal development. This can be a real aid towards improving performance and motivation.

When the training is over, try and evaluate its worth. Where do you expect to see improvements? If you evaluate effectively, you can judge where further investment in training will pay off.

The Secrets to Your Business' Success

Organizations of all sizes invest in their people through effective training. Your team is your most valuable asset and their performance has an impact on the company's bottom line.

All companies should review performance of their staff on a regular basis. When staff appraisals do not work, it is for the following reasons:

There is no system in place for undertaking reviews on a regular basis; there is no paper trail to follow so people don't know where to start; they are used purely to air grievances so become a negative thing; the appraiser isn't trained to appraise so the results are unreliable; there is no follow-up so improvements are missed.

About The Author

Ronan Knightly comes from a family of businessmen. At a very young age, he was already aware of how to plan, develop and manage a business. His father, Michael, made sure that Ronan understood the basic principles of being a successful businessman.

What his father failed to teach him was the importance of labor and how to be a great leader. Ronan is thirsty for knowledge as always; he studied the mastery of managing people as a key to a more blissful business.

www.ingramcontent.com/pod-product-compliance
Lightning Source LLC
Chambersburg PA
CBHW051254170526
45165CB00004B/1715